Written by Stef Reid

Illustrated by Philip Bannister

Contents

Collins

A challenging journey

I won a silver medal in the long jump at the London 2012 Paralympics. That one jump might seem a very simple thing to do, but my journey to the podium was not an easy one at all. The challenges I faced along the way were enough to make me want to give up – more than once – but that medal, and a few other amazing highlights, made the struggle well worth it. This is my story.

BT
Great CITYGAMES
REID
asics
MANCHESTER
adidas

My life was pretty exciting from the start. I was born in 1984 and had already lived in New Zealand and Hawaii by the age of three. At that point, it was just me and my sister, Samantha, who's three years older than me. My little brother, Scott, who's eight years younger, wasn't born yet.

Here I am with Samantha. I'm the one in the blue hat.

Honolulu, Hawaii

Toronto, Canada

Eventually, we moved to Toronto in Canada and it ended up being a permanent move. We were always a really active family and loved sports. My dad loved football in particular, so we played a lot of that. Sport is such a big part of life in Canada: at school we had PE every day. Life was great!

Sport from the start

My first real memory of organised sport was our school sports day, when I was six. I ran the sprint, the long-distance course and the relay and because I've always been a really competitive person, it just hooked me.

I'd start off in the autumn with cross-country running, then go into basketball, then volleyball. When I was older, I started track and rugby. It was great because I had a new sport every season. I really enjoyed being challenged. I like learning and I was lucky that we had such variety and so much opportunity.

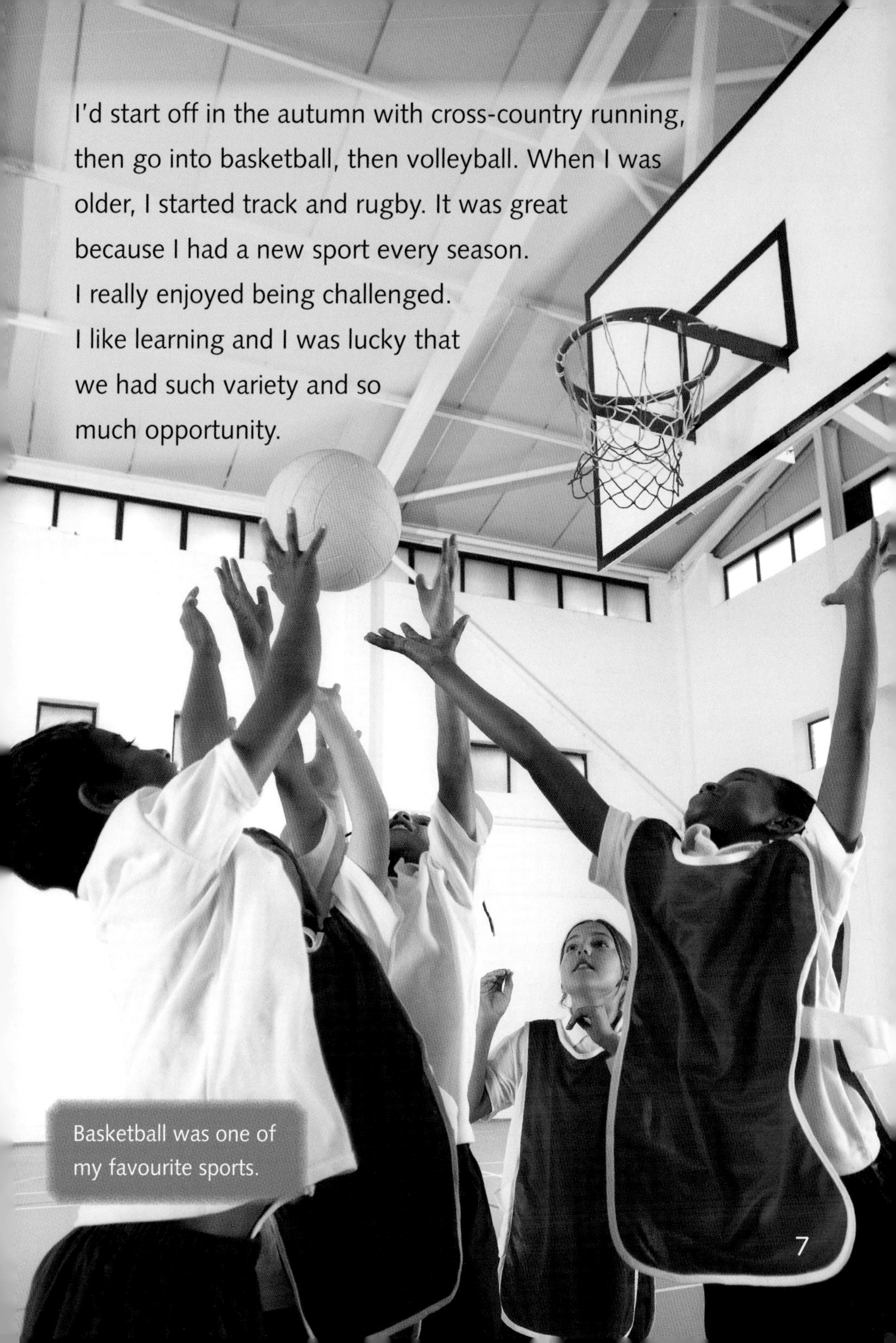

Basketball was one of my favourite sports.

There were tryouts for each team, but while my parents were happy for me to join school teams, they were really strict about studying, so I wasn't allowed to join teams outside of school. For them, education was the most important thing. Their standpoint was that you could do anything you wanted to at school, but that was it.

We practised throughout the week and had tournaments at the weekend, so for me sport was part of daily life. If there wasn't anything on, my brother Scott and I would play with the basketball net at home, kick about in the garden or play tag in the park.

Since I was small, I've always had this belief that if you're going to do something, you should do it to the best of your ability, or else what's the point? It doesn't matter if it's sport or a school test – if you don't win it's not the end of the world, but you may as well try.

I think I just realised early on that you can get attention in two ways, by being naughty and acting up, or by doing really well. My mum's a perfectionist and my dad's the biggest optimist in the world, and I think those two characteristics blended in a really positive way for me, so I'd always try very hard and no matter what happened I'd still go back with a positive attitude.

Discovering rugby

As a teenager, I started focusing on rugby. Our new PE teacher had played on the national team for Canada, so she introduced us to this cool new sport and put a team together. I was 12 when I started and I absolutely loved it! For me, there was nothing better than being on that field, covered in mud and running with the ball tucked under my arm, giving it my all.

It showcased everything I could do as an athlete. I was always quick, very **agile** and had tons of **endurance** – I could sprint up and down that field all day long. The second half of the game was the best for me because everyone else was tired, but I could just go on all day long.

I played scrum half, the link between the backs – the quick people who score – and the forwards – the bigger people who tackle. Although I'd probably have preferred to play back, because I liked scoring, I immediately knew that I'd found the sport for me. I still played other sports as well, but I knew then I wanted to play rugby internationally.

Rugby started to take up a lot of my time, as we trained four days a week after school and then would have one or two games on top of that. Sometimes I'd have tournaments at the weekend as well.

My parents were worried about me getting too involved in sport, because they wanted me to go to university. Even at 15, a few talent scouts watched me play and wanted me to shadow on the senior team. It was promising, but my parents made me focus on school, so that I remained balanced, and I'm thankful for that now.

At that point, my goal was to go to University in New Zealand and play rugby while I was there. Rugby is different in New Zealand – in Canada I was a big fish in a small pond and didn't come up against girls who were big and fast. I was the quickest on the field, so I never had to fear being tackled, but I knew in New Zealand there were going to be girls who had abilities I hadn't seen before.

The accident

When I was 16, I was invited up to my friends' cottage, just north of Toronto. I had such a fantastic time. We were right on the lake, so did a lot of water sports, including tubing, where you attach an inflated tube to the back of a motor boat and take off at a crazy speed. At the end of the weekend, just a couple of hours before leaving, we decided to go out on the boat one more time.

I hopped on the tube and away we went, but soon into the ride I fell off. I waited in the water for the boat to come back and pick me up, as it always did. I could see it coming from a distance, but as it got closer I knew something wasn't quite right; it was coming way too fast. I remember assessing my options – knowing I wouldn't be fast enough to swim away, I used my lifeguard training to decide that the best idea was to surface-dive and get as far below the surface of the water as possible, coming up only when I thought it was safe.

But I had completely forgotten that I had a life jacket on. The last thing I saw was the ridge of the front of the boat. I don't remember what happened after that, but when I came round the boat was a little way off. I didn't feel right, but couldn't figure out why. Then I looked at the water around me and it was completely red. I just lost it. I thought I'd been cut in half.

I remember reaching down my back and feeling skin flapping about. When I finally got on the boat I could see in everyone's faces that it was bad and nobody would let me look at my leg.

We were about three hours from a half-decent hospital, which was really scary. When we called for an ambulance they told us they weren't going to get there in time, so we just drove to the nearest clinic.

By that point someone had called my parents and they drove up. I remember seeing them, knowing they'd been sent into the clinic to say goodbye, but I just wasn't having it. I thought, this isn't going to end like this, I'm not done.

The biggest problem was the blood loss. The clinic didn't have any blood supplies and I had a massive gash along my back, which was about 20 centimetres deep. You can't just sew that up, plus the **propeller** blade had been dirty, so there was a high risk of infection.

I still had my life jacket on and that was holding everything in and together. Eventually the clinic stuck me in an ambulance, hoping that because I was young and fit, I might survive the long drive to the hospital.

I was terrified and thought I was going to die; that was all I could think about. I was so tired, so cold, but the ambulance driver told me not to sleep. This wave of exhaustion kept hitting me, but he'd tap me and explain that if I fell asleep I'd slip into a **coma** and wouldn't wake up again. They managed to call in one of the top surgeons in Canada and he met us at the best hospital in Toronto.

I don't remember getting to the hospital. The only thing I remember is waking up and seeing the doctor, who told me that everything had gone as well as it possibly could have and that there was no spinal damage.

I thought great, that was really lucky. Then my mum walked in. She looked really upset, but I didn't know why because I thought I'd just been given awesome news.

She told me that they'd had to **amputate** my foot at the ankle and I was absolutely devastated. I hadn't even really been aware of my foot injury – it wasn't a focus because my back was so bad and, although I knew I should just be happy to be alive, at that point I wasn't interested in life as an **amputee**.

To me, that was it, all I wanted to do was run and play sports – what was I going to do now? I was a 16-year-old girl and I didn't want to look different from my friends. I didn't even know any amputees.

Recovery – slow and steady

I was in hospital for about three weeks. I hated it; it was such a depressing place and everyone was sick. I didn't want to see anyone – I stopped caring and just wanted to sleep.

Things all changed, though, one Monday morning a week after the accident, when nurse Claudette came in with breakfast and I told her I wasn't hungry. So, big and cheery, she said, it was fine, that she'd help me to shower instead. I hadn't showered in a week, but I didn't really care about that either and told her I didn't feel like it. The next thing I knew, she'd slammed the tray down on my hospital bed and just looked me in the eye and told me that was enough, that I had to start doing something. It wasn't acceptable and I was better than that – my family was devastated and at least for them I should put on a smile and start doing something.

That shocked me. I was sick and I was a patient – how could she talk to me like that? But she caught my attention and was the first person who looked at me without feeling sorry for me. She wouldn't accept my bitterness; she wanted something better from me and that felt really good. She told me a story about a 12-year-old girl in the ward below who'd lost both her feet, but was still smiling and I was so competitive that it really bothered me that a 12-year-old was able to cope better than I could. It put things into perspective and reminded me that I was still the same person. I could have lost every single limb, but I'd still be the same competitive, determined, stubborn person.

At that point, I didn't know that I could still do sport, but I just thought, well, even if I couldn't do sport I'd channel my energy and determination into something else. You can still have goals and challenges and enjoy life. My life was going to be different to what I'd planned, but it wasn't over.

Back to school

When I got out of hospital
I had to walk using crutches
which, to my surprise, I loved.
They got me super-fit, and I
liked being in shape, so I'd go
everywhere on them. I couldn't
be fitted with an artificial leg
until all the scars had healed,
which took about three months,
so I was on my crutches
until then.

I wanted to get back to school
as soon as possible. When we
got out of hospital we went
to the school and made sure
I could get up and down
the stairs. Other than that,
I just sorted everything else
out as I went along.

It was strange going back to school and also intimidating, because the last thing I needed was people telling me how bad they felt for me. I just wanted to get on and pretend everything was normal.
My immediate friends got that, but other people who didn't really know me treated me like I was very fragile. They weren't sure how emotionally stable I was, so they treated me like I needed to be wrapped in cotton wool. It made me feel singled out and separated from everyone else – actually the last thing I wanted.

A sport-free life

The hardest thing for me was listening to our school announcements for tryouts for the basketball team. I couldn't play at that point and that was really tough. Our basketball coach had initially asked if I wanted to come along and score-keep, so I did for the first couple of games. But he could see from my face that it was a bad idea. Just having to sit there and watch from the sidelines was awful. I didn't want to watch other people playing, because I wanted to be out there too.

So, instead of sport I decided to try new things in the hour and a half after school before my mum finished work. I joined the drama club, the **trivia** team and the maths team. I became a 'mathlete' and was captain of the chess team. I think a lot of people focus on the things they can't do, but there are always a million things that you *can* do. What I was missing was that competitive outlet, so I found new ways to compete. I poured everything I had into studying and clubs and ended up top of the class.

Nurse Claudette changed my life. She changed my mindset, but that isn't to say I didn't have some bad days, especially when I first got my artificial leg. The weight of my body had to be held just below the knee and so, even though my stump was quite long, the safest place for the artificial leg to start was below the knee.

I hated my first **prosthetic** leg. Because I was an athlete I had really big calves, which meant that my artificial leg had to be big and clunky. It was probably the ugliest prosthetic leg I've had, but when you first become an amputee, for about the first five years your **prosthesis** is changed every six months to make it a good fit, because the shape of your stump changes. My big calf became very skinny because I couldn't use the muscle any more, but even as it changed and the fit of the artificial leg got better and better, it took me about four years before I was really comfortable with my body and how it looked.

I'd thought I would be able to put my artificial leg on and just walk off, not realising that my bones wouldn't be strong enough yet. The bones needed a chance to build up to take the weight, so my stump swelled up inside the prosthesis. It was incredibly painful; I couldn't even get the prosthesis off, it was so swollen.

So, it wasn't smooth sailing. It was a process and I learnt to be kind to myself and let people know that there were going to be some tantrums, and that I might need a quiet corner for ten minutes. I just did whatever I had to do, let it out, then came back and tried again. I think that was the best thing I did, just let the emotions out. I never held anything back, which was actually a really healthy way to deal with it. Initially, I walked with crutches, then with a cane. My goal was to be able to dance without a cane by New Year. And I did – I was walking within two months.

Everyone expected me to get back into sport the minute I walked in the school. The rugby teacher offered to open the pool for me in the afternoon, but I just wanted to be left alone. I was scared to have confirmation that I wasn't as good as I used to be. In a sense, the hope was better than the reality, so I'd rather not do it, not know, and still have hope. My volleyball coach had asked me to go to a game and I just said, I can't! I can't run – what am I going to do? She suggested that she just sub me in to serve and then she'd take me out, so I agreed. I loved serving anyway and that was the best part of my game. I served and waited for her to take me out, but she just left me.

So I got into position, but because everyone had been telling me for months and months that I was injured, all I could think about was being broken and hurt. I was frozen with fear that the ball would come to me, but when it was thrown to the girl behind me, without thinking, I took off after it. I didn't get there, but it didn't matter because at that moment I realised that I could still do it and the only thing stopping me was thinking that I couldn't, and of course a few practical realities that I'd get sorted. That was when I realised that I'd get back; I didn't know when, but I'd get back.

Trying again

I went back to playing rugby about eight months after the accident, by which time I had my first artificial running leg. However, because my stump couldn't take much pressure, at the beginning I could only run for about ten minutes once a week before it started hurting – I'd storm to the end of the field, take the leg off and just sit and cry. It was very painful and frustrating; it wasn't a glorious return, to be honest. If I didn't love running as much as I did, I don't know if I would have stayed with it. I'd have picked something like swimming or biking, which didn't have the same **impact**. But I wanted to run.

Even now when people ask me about running, the reality is, I wouldn't recommend it as a first-choice activity for an amputee. You've got to really love it. It still causes a lot of problems with my body – my back especially. I have to commit totally to it, otherwise I'm just going to end up at a point where I'm struggling to walk and I plan to keep walking all my life.

Before the accident, my attitude was very much "education first", but things changed a bit afterwards. Sport become important for other reasons; it became about me getting my life back. It wasn't about me becoming a superstar or wanting to be a professional athlete; I just wanted my life back and my parents were really supportive. But, because I didn't know about the Paralympics, I'd accepted that sport was going to play a much more **recreational** role.

Moving on

I graduated from high school wanting to be a doctor. I was so impressed with what the doctors had done for me after the accident and I'd always loved the idea of surgery. I just knew I wanted to do something significant and challenging with my life and doctors help people in a really practical way. So I went off to university and about three weeks into my first year, I saw my first track and field practice. I was watching it from my dorm room while studying and I just remember sitting there wondering how fast I still was.

So I gave the coach, Wayne, a call and explained the situation. He was so **gracious** and told me that if I was committed and came every day, he'd train me. Usually at the end of the first month they cut the team and only those who make time standards will move on, but he explained that he'd train me for the full four years on campus.

Pulled back to sport

Track and field is made up of a range of activities: sprint, long distance and field events such as long jump and throwing. Initially, I was training to be a sprinter. I wanted to do 60, 100 and 200 metres. I'll never forget the very first practice I went to – we were on the track for about 50 minutes, doing all sorts of drills, and I was absolutely exhausted, sitting by the water bottles.

It had been really tough, but I'd got through it. Then Wayne came round and said the warm-up was over – the session would start in about five minutes and I just thought, "You've got to be kidding!"

I trained three times a week at the track from about 7 o'clock to 9 o'clock in the evening, then I'd weightlift two other days a week.

I was the only person in the team with a disability. The others were fine with it – it was me more than anyone who had the problem. I was still not entirely comfortable with myself, as I was so used to being super-confident and going out on the field knowing I was the best, but now I was in a position where I was no longer the best. I was the worst by far and it was really hard to deal with that; it was a very **humbling experience**. I spent a lot of my time in that initial period feeling very uncomfortable, assuming that everyone else thought I didn't deserve to be there.

It's sad because I could have enjoyed those first two years a lot more than I did, but I was so uncomfortable with myself and what I could do that it spoilt them for me. Fortunately, by my fourth year I'd got over that and built up a lot more confidence. I'd learnt about the Paralympics and realised that I didn't have to keep racing these guys and losing to them. If I have one regret, it's spending those two years feeling bad about myself when there was absolutely no need to.

My first competition was actually a disability event. I'd done some research and found the Ontario Paralympics Championships, so I went to that in the summer of 2003. I'd never seen so many disabled people in all my life. They weren't all amputees; there were a lot of wheelchair racers, people with visual impairment, or cerebral palsy. I competed in the 100 and 800 metres. I didn't have a clue what I was doing; I just ran and won both events. Suddenly, my world was transformed.

A bit of focus and huge success

In my third year of university, I transferred from Queen's University to the University of Windsor, which had an amazing track team. They had an **elite** disability course there and I knew that if I wanted to get better at track and field, that's where I needed to be.

the running track, University of Windsor

If I was going to go anywhere with sport, I needed to spend a year focusing on it and so I did – great decision. When I went back to Queen's for my fourth year I'd improved so much that I got to compete with the able-bodied. We'd had really, really good coaching at Windsor, with the result that my body had toughened up and I was able to handle a higher volume of training. I was also a lot more confident, not being the only disabled person there. Once that confidence was there, it was solid, and although I wasn't the best runner, instead of finishing last, I was finishing mid-pack. I remember coming second in a 400-metre race at Harvard and that was quite incredible.

In April 2006, I got my first invite to an international event in England – not to run, but to take part in the long jump. So I called the long-jump coach at Queen's and he trained me up a bit for the event.

We only had time for a couple of long jump sessions before the competition, but, amazingly, at my first real elite disabled event I came fourth.

Then that summer I made the world championship team in Aston. I finished sixth in the long jump and seventh in both the 100 and 200 metres. Again, it was an eye-opener, because the difference between first and seventh was huge and it made me realise that I needed to start training like the other competitors if I wanted to beat them. I couldn't just train part-time anymore – I was going to have to *really* train.

I had to make a decision about whether to continue with medical school, or try to make the 2008 Beijing Paralympics team. I knew I couldn't do both, so I decided to go for the sport. I felt I'd come too far to take the safe route – I wanted at least to give it a shot.

I moved to the University of Windsor and started training more with my long jump coach, which had become my focus event.

I still wanted to sprint, but we realised that I was more gifted at long jump, probably because I'm really agile. It's fun too, less intense than the 100 metres, where you've got one shot and that's it. With the sprint, you're out on the track, on stage so to speak, for about two minutes, whereas with the long jump you can have a lot more fun with the crowd. They're more chilled-out, so are the competitors, and the **atmosphere** is great.

Standards are published for the Paralympics, so you can work out for yourself where you lie. In my mind, I knew I was going to Beijing. I had made the standards enough times that getting selected wasn't going to be an issue, but, in fact, the two months before were really, really rough.

I was at practice one evening and we were doing some jumping drills. I was being really keen and thought, I'll just do one more, which wasn't listed in my programme. I came down on my ankle really poorly, probably because of **fatigue**. I ended up with a terrible sprained ankle, so wasn't able to train much. It was stressful because I knew my lead-up to the trials wasn't ideal, which was rather scary.

However, I still got selected for the team and went to the training camp in Switzerland for two weeks before the Games. It's good to get out of your normal environment and just relax a bit, away from all the stress. Everyone thought I was going to win the long jump and probably break the world record while doing it, so the pressure was huge.

members of the Canadian Paralympic team

National Stadium, Beijing

The long jump was my first event and at 9 o'clock in the morning. I walked out into the stadium, in front of 80,000 people. I'd never in my life been at an event with more than 5,000 people spectating, so it just blew my mind. I was so nervous and I wanted it so badly that it made me really tense and you just can't compete like that – you've got to be confident and relaxed. I think because I had so much adrenalin in my body I was running much harder than I normally would. I just wanted to try so hard, but sometimes trying hard is the worst thing you can do. You've just got to let it happen and trust that it's going to.

I tried too hard in the long jump.

As a result, I had five fouls out of my six attempts and was sitting in last place. I was absolutely devastated and I remember thinking that I'd completely blown it. Then I put in one last jump, which was a really safe jump. I ended up in a tie for fourth place and that was it. I went back to the athletes' village and cried for two hours, but the worst part was that I still had the 200-metre final to come that evening.

I was devastated, because I knew that my medal shot was gone. I wasn't quick enough in the 100 or 200 metres to get a medal; the long jump had been my only shot. So I had to come to terms with that before the next event and decide that all I could do was my best. So this time when I went out, instead of being tense and nervous, I decided just to enjoy it. I waved to the crowd, looked at the camera and had fun.

We got in our blocks and I was in lane nine; lane nine is where the slow people go, but I just went for it. I had a great start, a good corner, but even so I was only sitting in sixth place. Then out of the corner of my eye I saw the leader trip and fall, then she took out the girl next to her.

Suddenly I was sitting in fourth place and knew that this would never happen again. I had to go all out and just like that my speed doubled and I ended up getting a bronze. It was crazy; it was the last thing I thought would happen. I learnt a very good lesson, though, because if I hadn't committed from the start of the race and thought, "I'm just going to do my best," I wouldn't have been in the position to take advantage of what happened.

It felt surreal. In some ways, I thought that I didn't really deserve it and it was kind of hard to accept. But on the other hand, I was also incredibly proud and thankful – after all, I'd walked away with a PB (Personal Best), a good finish and a medal!

The race leaders tripped and fell.

the 100 metres final

The 100 metres was four days later and was a total disaster. With all the excitement, I just couldn't get my head back in the right place and I didn't even make the final. Looking back, we should have held off celebrating until after everything was done, because it put me in the wrong mind-set. But at the time, that just wasn't possible. When I was lying in that hospital bed eight years before, getting a medal in front of a crowd of 80,000 people was the last thing I thought I'd ever do, but here I was, living out my dream, which I'd been convinced I'd have to give up. It was really cool.

I received a bronze medal.

Beijing helped me to gain a lot of confidence in myself – just the fact that I'd been able to perform in the 200 metres after such devastation in the long jump and under so much pressure. It was also the first time I began to see that sport might be a viable career for me.

Onwards and upwards

The following year, I broke the long jump world record at a really small event, just north of London. My coach and I were simply going out there to work on my technique, with no intention of doing anything special. Then I just popped out this jump and when it was announced that I'd broken the world record, I couldn't believe it. I'd had a really devastating 100-metre race in the Paris Grand Prix only two weeks before and had felt so frustrated. I'd run very poorly in Paris and couldn't see the point any more, then this world record suddenly happened. It was hugely encouraging and, a week and a half later, I broke it twice more in one week.

This time, it was made extra special because my family were there to see it. My mum, sister and brother were in town and it was just so cool to celebrate my success with them.

For me, it was just immense personal satisfaction. I'd worked so hard and sometimes you wonder if you're wasting your time, but it confirmed that hard work matters. I'm pretty hard on myself and I come with a lot of determination, but it wasn't about investing more hours in training, it was about making each hour count that little bit more. Part of that comes from really believing in yourself and building up confidence. It takes a lot of energy to achieve this – I had so many gremlins in my head constantly telling me that I wasn't good enough, that I might as well quit, that it took a lot of work to stay positive.

The power of positive thinking

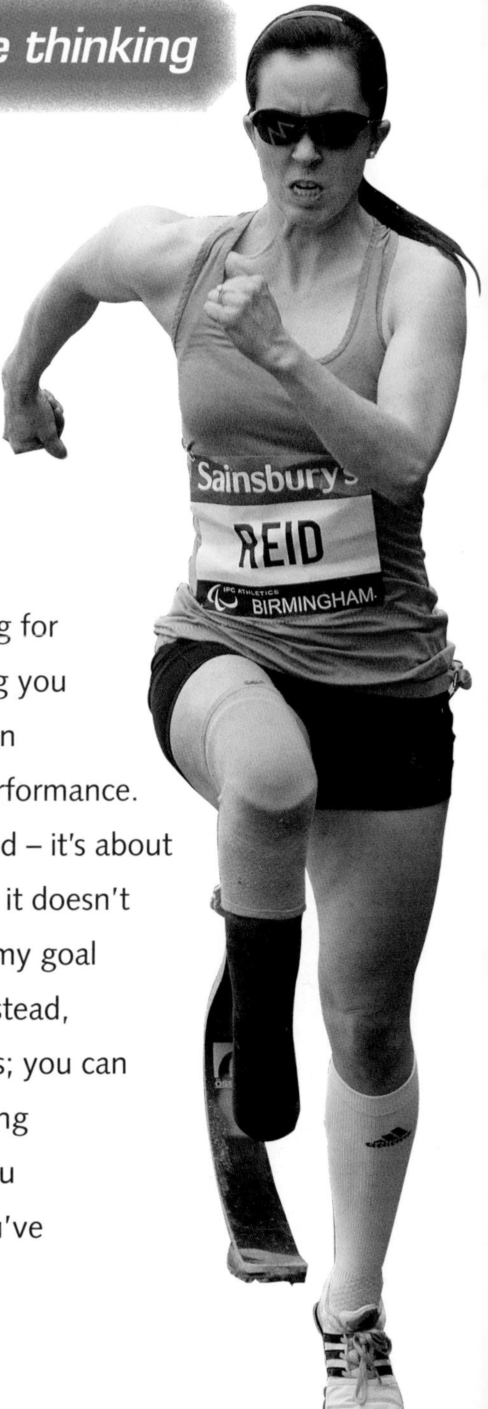

You've got to believe that you're going to win. You've got to go in confident and relaxed and use the facts of your success. When your mind is telling you that you can't do it, actually you know you can and that's a powerful thing.

It's hard to go into an event aiming for gold, because that's not something you can control. The only thing you can control on the day is your own performance. My goals are therefore time-related – it's about getting the best time for me, then it doesn't matter what anyone else does. If my goal was to get gold and I got silver instead, I would feel bad. That's dangerous; you can get really caught up with comparing yourself to other people, when you should always celebrate when you've done well.

A person next to me isn't going to affect me in my lane. I'm on my own on that runway. I have a vague idea of where I'm sitting in the competition and I have strategies of how I'm going to jump – a plan. I usually do a safe jump first, then I've got five jumps to play around. Everybody gets three jumps, but after three jumps only the top 12 move on to the final and then you get another three jumps. After the first three jumps, they reorder you, so the person with the shortest jump goes first and the person leading goes last.

After that third jump you know where you are, but I don't like watching the other competitors; I don't care what they do. I lie on the track with a towel over my head and just try to chill out. It's important to live in the moment, not to get too far ahead of yourself.

I have a mentor who encourages me to write down five things that I'm thankful for every morning when I wake up. They can be absolutely ridiculous, like peanut butter, but it changes your mind-set for the rest of the day. It puts you in a mood where you're thinking positively and, no matter where you are, you're looking for positives as opposed to things that are bad.

Sometimes I'll bring that piece of paper to the track and read through those things and think, "Yes, this is a good day." Your mind is so powerful; my coach says 80 per cent of the competition happens above the shoulders.

At the New Zealand World Championships in 2011, I won two bronze medals, one in the long jump and one in the 200 metres. I was definitely feeling more confident. It was the first chance I'd had since Beijing to practise what it was like to compete over a longer period of time and the last chance before the London Paralympics.

So for me it was about the mental longevity, keeping things together, staying focused. I came away with a PB in the 100 metres, I was a bit below standard in the long jump, and the 200 metres was great in terms of getting a third-place medal – I wasn't expecting a medal in the sprints, so it was a really good feeling.

Injured and down and out

The year after all that success was really tough. I ended up with about seven stress fractures throughout my body, six in my foot and one really serious one in my back. I didn't run for about five months and was cycling instead, to the point where I'd decided that if I wasn't running in another month I'd try out for the Paralympics cycle team.

But it was hard and I wasn't in a good place. I knew something had to change, so in January 2012, eight months before the Paralympics, I changed my coach. Everyone thought I was crazy, but that is what I needed to do, so I went for it, and it was the best thing I could have done. I'd rather take the risk of changing coach and have it work out horribly than stay still, knowing that I wouldn't perform well.

But even as I improved, I knew my competitors had five months on me. That's a long time; you can't get those five months back, all you can do is commit yourself to every single session that you have left and that's what I did.

My new coach was a really great communicator. He could look at me and know the problem. He was all about playing with my mind-set – getting me into a much more positive, confident state. That was his goal and he did a good job.

The London 2012 Paralympics

In terms of qualification for the London Paralympics, there were A standards and B standards and you had to make two A standards the year before the Games to get on the team. It was stressful, but I knew that based on my criteria I was going to make it.

We found out at the end of June. The team is deliberately picked that close because the selectors want people who are peaking at the right point. If they picked the team earlier, they'd have no idea what the competitors would deliver at the Games. So I went off to the holding camp in Portugal for 12 days and it was great.

the Paralympic Village, London

People arrived at the Paralympic Village in London three or four days before their event. You don't want to get there too early because the Village is actually an incredibly stressful place – you're surrounded by people who are nervous about their own events, so it's a very tense environment.

We were in a town house with three double bedrooms and two singles. I was in a single, so if I needed to be alone, I just went upstairs and closed my door.

My first race was the 100 metres. I ran fairly well, just outside my PB, so that was good. Again, I went into the Games knowing that my shot at gold was in the long jump. I wasn't going to win gold in the 100 or 200 metres, so my coach didn't want my first experience to be the long jump, as it was in Beijing. He wanted me to get out there, get the nerves out and become used to the stadium before the high-pressured event.

So we did the 100 metres and it went well – actually, it was awesome. The crowd support was just **phenomenal**.

I ran well in the 100 metres heat.

It was a million times better than Beijing. It wasn't scary at all and I felt so at home, with the crowd cheering me on because I'm British. It didn't matter where I came in the race, the crowd was just proud of me and it was like a big hug with 80,000 people who wanted to share my passion, share the experience and watch me do my best. It was really cool, I loved it and was so excited for the long jump.

I'd made the 100-metre final, then the next morning it was the long jump, which was the one I really cared about. Because I'm a below-the-knee amputee and I was competing with above-the-knee amputees, I was obviously going to jump further – you're not going to be as fast if you don't have a knee. The scoring is done on a points system; for example, for me to get 1,000 points, I'd need to jump five metres, but an above-the-knee amputee would need to jump 20 per cent less to get the same points. I'd never competed like that before, so I didn't know how things were going to pan out and sometimes it was confusing; my mum thought I was winning the whole time because I was jumping the farthest!

In the end, it was down to me and one other athlete – Kelly Cartwright, an Australian. I was winning, then she was winning, then I was winning, then she was winning. On my fifth jump, I jumped the furthest I'd ever done, but it was fouled. I was devastated.

I'd just stepped over the line – half an inch over and that was the difference between a silver and a gold medal. I still had one more jump left and I gave it everything I had, but it just didn't pay off, so my initial reaction to the silver medal was disappointment.

I received a silver medal.

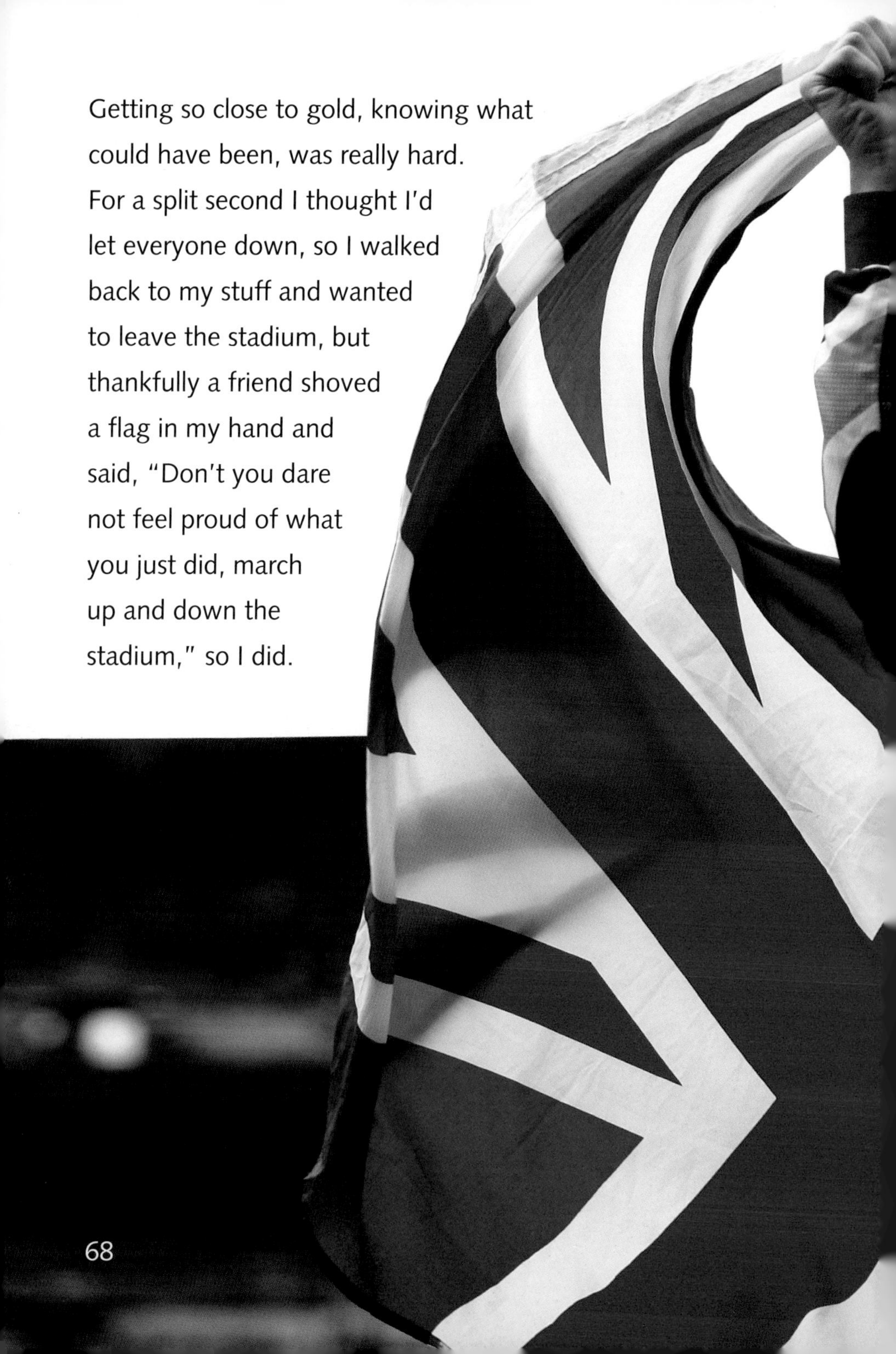

Getting so close to gold, knowing what could have been, was really hard. For a split second I thought I'd let everyone down, so I walked back to my stuff and wanted to leave the stadium, but thankfully a friend shoved a flag in my hand and said, "Don't you dare not feel proud of what you just did, march up and down the stadium," so I did.

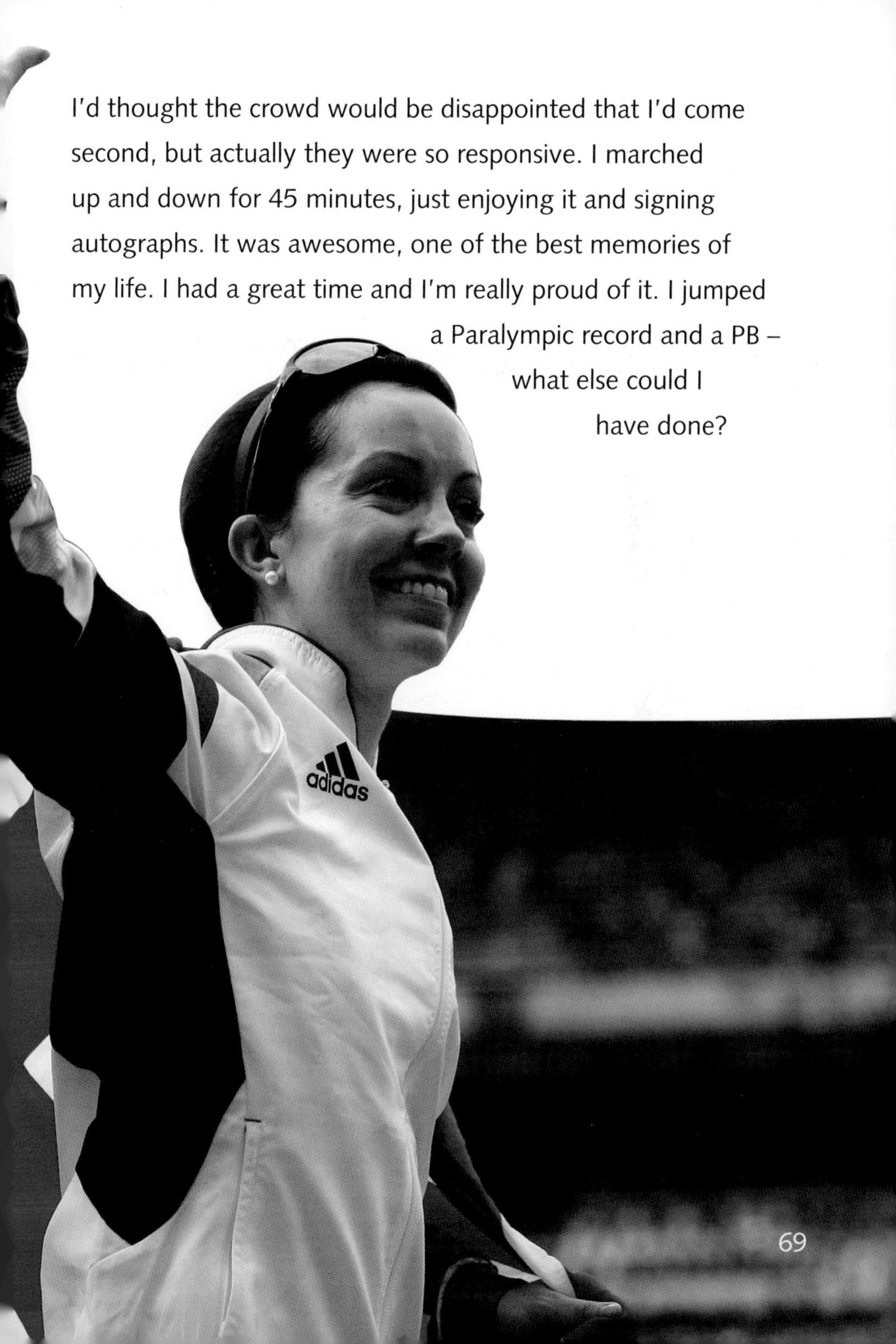

I'd thought the crowd would be disappointed that I'd come second, but actually they were so responsive. I marched up and down for 45 minutes, just enjoying it and signing autographs. It was awesome, one of the best memories of my life. I had a great time and I'm really proud of it. I jumped a Paralympic record and a PB – what else could I have done?

That evening it was the 100-metre final. It was a terrible race and I came last, but again I just had to accept that I'm only human. I was exhausted from the morning and not all the girls had done both events. It wasn't that I was just physically tired, but mentally as well.

the 100 metres final

Straight after the long jump, I'd had to prepare for this race and although I was leading after ten metres, I just couldn't hold it together. That's the reality of competing in three different events. I couldn't have done any better; for me, excellence is doing the best that I can on the day. If I can honestly say that I have done my best, then wherever I finish is worth celebrating.

I still had to compete in the 200 metres a few days later, so we went back to the Village and **recouped**. I was really nervous about the 200 metres, because we'd had some problems with my prosthesis when running around the corner and I didn't have the fitness behind me that I needed, so it was hard going into a race knowing I wasn't at my **prime**. But my coach said he didn't care what happened in the race as long as I went for it, which I did and it was incredible fun. I ended up coming fourth with another PB, so again I was really proud and it was a great way to end my Paralympics.

the 200 metres heats

I stood on the track for a little while afterwards and just enjoyed it. When I walked off through the media zone, one interviewer seemed really disappointed for me, but the truth was that I was **elated**. That day, I'd learnt what would define personal excellence for me; I'd never give that job to anyone else and I think that's a good lesson.

I remember sitting in my room after it was all over, just looking at this medal and finding myself asking whether it had all been worth it, everything I'd given up to win it. It was a hard question to answer – it wasn't an immediate yes. But I thought about it and while I realised that it hadn't by any means been a perfect four years – the journey, the experience and the struggles had changed who I was. I wasn't the same person I'd been four years before, so, yes, I think it was worth it. But it was weird … post-Paralympic blues maybe!

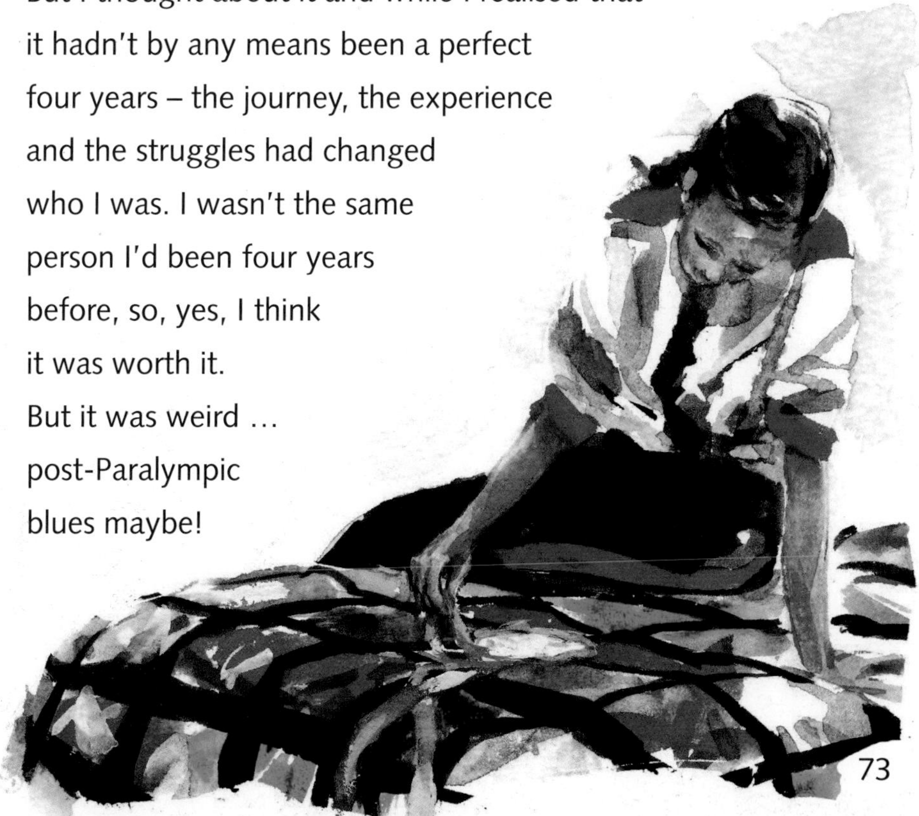

Where next?

As a result of the Paralympics, my life has now changed so much and I get these wonderful opportunities to meet people and do different things. For now, I'm just trying new **ventures**. I'm going to have a shot at a speaking career and I've developed a nutrition bar for athletes. I have a policy not to say no to anything and eventually an opportunity will come by which will be a perfect fit.

I'd love to go to the Rio 2016 Paralympics – I'm going to train for it, but Paralympic sport changes so much every year, with new people coming up. I think I'll still be competitive at that time, but we'll have to wait and see. There are a lot of girls coming through who want my place, but I'll fight for it as long as I can. In May 2014 I managed a long jump of 5.45m in Clermont to break the world record. I had known I could do it, and I celebrated, but it still wasn't an end goal – there's always more I can achieve, if I work hard enough.

A big struggle, a huge reward

My experience as an amputee has been so positive and a lot of that was because I had access to so many different resources. Prosthetic legs are very expensive, mainly because of the socket, which needs to be a perfect fit. I'm lucky enough to have lots of different amazing legs for different purposes. I have an everyday leg, a swimming leg, a high-heeled leg and a ski leg, which fits into a ski boot, though my running leg is the one that's most important to me. I've always had a wonderful support environment, but the experience of someone who doesn't is vastly different.

If someone asked me whether I'd rather have my old foot back, yes, of course I would – nothing beats the real thing. But I've learnt so much and while they've not been fun at the time, the best parts in life are the struggles. You've got to experience hardship and pain for something to really have meaning and I wouldn't trade my struggle, my dream, for anything.

Glossary

agile	able to move quickly and easily
amputate	to cut off a limb by surgery
amputee	a person who has had a limb amputated
atmosphere	the mood of a place
coma	a state of deep unconsciousness
elated	extremely happy
elite	people who are the best at something
endurance	lots of energy and stamina
fatigue	extreme tiredness
gracious	courteous and generous
humbling experience	being made to feel less important
impact	pressure on the body
phenomenal	extraordinary
prime	the best someone can be at something
propeller	broad angled blades attached to a revolving shaft that drive boats and aeroplanes
prosthetic	artificial
prosthesis	an artificial body part
recouped	regained lost energies
recreational	for enjoyment, not competition
trivia	things of very little importance
ventures	new undertakings

Index

My journey to the London 2012 Paralympics

1984

I was born in New Zealand.

1988

My family moved to Toronto, Canada.

1996

I started to play rugby at school.

2000

My right foot was amputated after a boating accident.

2003

I went to Queen's University to study to be a doctor.

I took part in the Ontario Paralympics Championships.

I made the World Championships team in Aston.

I broke the long-jump world record in London.

I won silver at the London Paralympics.

2006

2009

2012

2008

2011

2014

I won bronze at the Beijing Paralympics.

I won two bronze medals at the New Zealand World Championships.

I broke the long-jump world record.

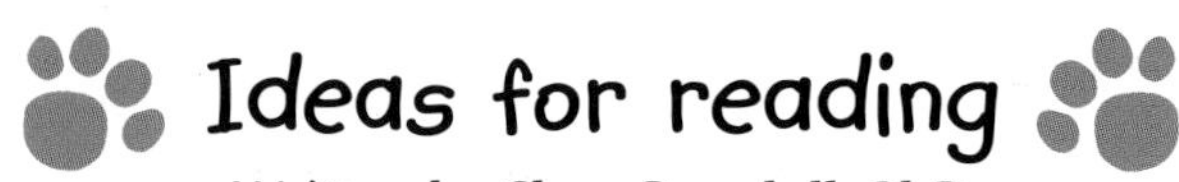

Ideas for reading

Written by Clare Dowdall, PhD
Lecturer and Primary Literacy Consultant

Learning objectives: draw inferences such as inferring characters' feelings, thoughts and motives; retrieve, record and present information from non-fiction; note and develop initial ideas, drawing on reading and research where necessary; use spoken language to develop understanding through speculating, hypothesizing, imagining and exploring ideas

Curriculum links: PE

Interest words: agile, amputate, amputee, elite, impact, prosthetic, prosthesis

Resources: ICT

Getting started

This book can be read over two or more reading sessions.

- Ask children to recount their memories of the London 2012 Paralympic Games, and to share any knowledge of disabled athletes' achievements and challenges.
- Hand out the book and read the title and blurb. Check that children know what an autobiography is. Help them to notice the features of an autobiography from the blurb, e.g. it is written in the first person, it describes events that happened from a personal perspective.

Reading and responding

- Ask children to read through the contents to construct a picture of Stef Reid's life, interests and achievements from the information provided. Discuss how the contents can help children to read for information.
- Ask children to read to p13, to learn about Stef before her accident. As they read, ask them to look for the qualities and opportunities that contributed to her becoming a successful athlete.
- Ask children to read on to find out about her accident, recovery and ultimate success.